Ultimate FACTIVITY Co

Find out all about LEGO® Friends with fun, fascinating activities that help you learn as you play. All the activities can be done right on the page, you just need a few coloring pencils and some imagination!

Contents

This book belongs to:

_____

Meet Stephanie, Andrea, Mia, Olivia, and Emma. They love spending time together. Whether they are working on an exciting project, going on an adventure, or just hanging out, they always have fun!

Mia

Animal-lover Mia is a very caring person. She is always on hand to listen to her friends' problems and will do everything she can to help.

Emma

Creative Emma will design anything! From posters and bags to her friends' clothes and bedrooms. She wants everything to look beautiful.

Andrea

Andrea loves being the center of attention and entertaining her friends. She is good at giving them confidence to try new things.

Stephanie

Energetic Stephanie loves baking cakes, playing soccer, and organizing parties. She is always encouraging her friends to get involved in new activities.

Hanging out

It's never quiet when the friends hang out together. Mia shows Emma and Andrea her new drum set. They can't wait to have a go!

At the pool

On a hot summer's day, the girls love cooling down at Olivia's splash pool. They chat and laugh over cool drinks under the umbrella.

Emma's house

Emma's friends love spending time at her house. They relax in the living room and plan their next adventures from Emma's cool bedroom.

Olivia

Brainy Olivia can be shy, but around her friends she's lots of fun! Olivia loves inventing things and often creates cool gadgets for her friends.

Find the **stickers** at the back of the book.

Favorite Hobbies

Match the equipment to its owner

Everyone enjoys a hobby! Whether you love sports or swimming, a hobby is a great way to make the most of your free time—and it's good exercise too! You need the right equipment for your hobby.

What's your favorite hobby?

Work out which equipment belongs to which friend. Next, draw the equipment in the friend's hand.

Go team!

Stephanie

Stephanie loves playing team sports. She runs **long distances** to keep fit and practices by kicking the ball at a **target**. Last match, Stephanie scored three goals!

Kate

Kate's favorite hobby is **snorkeling**, where she looks at fish and coral as she swims in the ocean. Kate needs a mask to see underwater, and must **kick** her legs powerfully.

Skis

Skis are attached to the bottom of shoes or boots, to help you move fast over **snow**. It take a lot of practice to stay **upright** as you ski down a slope.

Basketball

Basketball players try to capture this large ball from the **opposing team** as they run across the court. Then they must **throw** the ball through a hoop to score points.

Use a **pencil** to **sketch** the equipment first.

Olivia

Olivia's hobby requires a good sense of **balance** and lots and lots of practice! Her equipment needs to be **sturdy** enough to ride over strong ocean waves.

Time to practice again!

Matthew

Sporty Matthew has always loved **competitive** sports. He is really good at throwing the ball through the hoop because he has **excellent aim**. Matthew is also a great team player.

Christina

Christina enjoys **winter** sports because she loves feeling the icy wind in her hair as she zips down a mountain. Her hobby requires strong, **steady legs** and lot of balance.

Surfboard

This **strong** surfboard is designed to stay **right-side-up** on the powerful ocean waves so its rider doesn't fall in too much!

Flippers

Flippers are big, flat shoes for wearing in water. They make each kick **stronger**, so that the swimmer moves faster, with less effort, and **less splashing**.

Soccer ball

Soccer players chase the soccer ball across a **large pitch** toward the opposing team's goal. They must **kick** the ball into the goal to score.

Find the **answers** on page 97.

Working Together
Write in the speech bubbles

Working together isn't always easy. Andrea and Stephanie are the best of friends and they like to be the center of attention. They are both loud, and they both love voicing their opinions. Sometimes, this can lead to a disagreement.

What **title** will you give your story?

Decide what each character will say and write it in the blank speech bubbles.

You could write in **pencil** first and then use a **pen**.

Stephanie and Andrea are organizing a charity event.

Excited, they go off on their own to get started with the planning...

Stephanie asks her other friends if they want to help out.

Andrea writes a blog post to start getting the word out.

Both Stephanie and Andrea have an idea about the official entertainment...

I'm going to perform a dance.

But I was going to sing a song.

Oh dear! Sounds like there might be a bit of a problem...

Olivia has a bright idea, which might just save the day.

The night of the talent show has arrived...

THE END!

7

Various Vehicles
Match the drivers and vehicles

The girls drive all sorts of vehicles—each for a different purpose. Some are for rescuing animals or delivering supplies, others can be driven over difficult terrain.

Read about the different vehicles. Use the clues to identify each driver and find the correct sticker.

I transport things in my vehicle.

My vehicle has wheels of different sizes.

There is a sidecar on my vehicle.

Beach Buggy

Olivia's Beach Buggy has large, off-road tires for a smooth ride over the sand dunes. There is also enough space at the back to hold her surfing equipment.

Eco Car

Mia's pretty blue Eco Car has lots of environmentally friendly features. It uses less gas than a regular car and can even run on electricity for a short while!

First Aid Bike

Emma uses her First Aid Bike to transport medical supplies or injured animals. The bike and its small sidecar travel easily over narrow jungle paths.

Convertible

Stephanie's Convertible is perfect for a lovely day out. It has enough space to carry picnic supplies or a dog-grooming kit —whatever Stephanie needs for her latest adventure.

1 I drive the:

_____

_____

My vehicle is purple.

↓

There is space in the trunk for my stuff.

↓

My vehicle has a cool orange star on it.

↓

?

My vehicle has large, strong wheels.

↓

It has two yellow headlamps.

↓

There is enough space for a surfboard.

↓

?

My vehicle is blue.

↓

I use a lot less gas in this vehicle.

↓

My vehicle has two white headlamps.

↓

?

2 I drive the:

✎ _____

_____

3 I drive the:

✎ _____

_____

4 I drive the:

✎ _____

_____

Find the **stickers** at the back of the book.

Find the **answers** on page 97.

Inventing

Design a robot friend for Zobo

Olivia spends lots of time in her Invention Workshop, designing clever gadgets, apps, and computer programs. Her latest creation is a cute little robot called Zobo, who can help Olivia out with many things.

Read about Olivia's robot Zobo, then design your own robot.

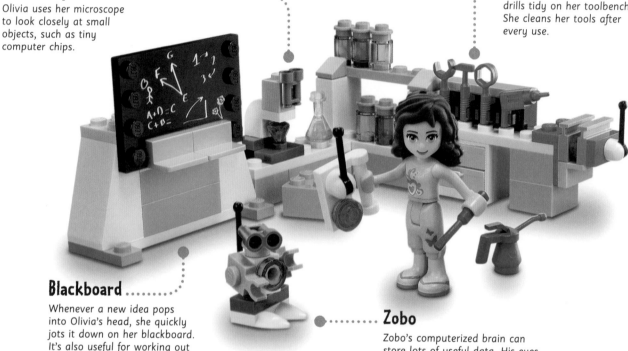

Microscope
Olivia uses her microscope to look closely at small objects, such as tiny computer chips.

Toolbench
Olivia keeps her wrenches, hammers, spanners, and drills tidy on her toolbench. She cleans her tools after every use.

Blackboard
Whenever a new idea pops into Olivia's head, she quickly jots it down on her blackboard. It's also useful for working out math problems.

Zobo
Zobo's computerized brain can store lots of useful data. His eyes are fitted with cameras and his mechanical hands are designed to function as various tools too!

Remote control   Smartphone   Oil can   Chemicals

Invention Workshop

Olivia's workshop is filled with tools and gadgets to help and inspire her. Olivia likes to collect interesting things, because they might be useful one day.

Draw lightly in **pencil** first, then use **colored pens** or **pencils** to complete your robot.

Will your robot have **arms** and **legs**? Or will it have wheels?

Think about what your **robot** will be able to do. What **tools** will it need?

Choose a cool **color scheme** for your robot.

My robot's name is: _____

Perfect Pets

Spot the dog

The girls meet lots of adorable animals in their day-to-day lives. Some of the girls even have more than one pet. But they are all agreed: nothing is cuter than a playful puppy pal!

Work out which pet belongs to which friend. Find the stickers at the back of the book.

Emma

Emma loves creating new looks for her pretty white poodle. At the last makeover, her dog especially loved her new pink, buckled collar!

Olivia

Olivia's friendly brown dog has long brown ears and dreamy blue eyes. Olivia thinks she looks beautiful with a blue bow to match her eyes.

Andrea

Andrea's smiley, light brown dog is very curious. Andrea loves taking him for walks. She is proud of how cute he looks with his new blue bow!

Stephanie

Stephanie spends lots of time with this adventurous brown puppy. She loves stroking the puppy's short brown ears!

Mia

Mia and her goofy white pup always have such fun. Mia loves the brown patch around her dog's eye. It's so cute!

Marie

Marie's white poodle keeps her company at the City Park Café. Marie loves her pet's gorgeous green eyes and purple collar!

A girl's best friend

Charlie

Charlie is full of fun. He loves making everyone laugh.

Celie

Loyal poodle Celie's favorite foods are pies and cakes.

Coco

Coco is cute and mischievous. He loves splashing in water.

Lady

Lady wags her tail when she wears her favorite pink collar.

Scarlett

Playful Scarlett likes learning new tricks and just having fun.

Max

Max likes to discover new places—it helps him make new friends!

Find the **answers** on page 97.

Fabulous Fashion

Create a new outfit

Emma is extremely creative. She loves making things look beautiful—especially clothes! Emma is always coming up with new fashion ideas. When designing for her friends, she keeps their individual styles in mind.

Read about the girls' outfits. Then design a new outfit for Emma.

Design studio

Emma has her own design studio at home. She has lots of drawers filled with amazing fabrics and accessories, and a mood board, where she pins up anything that inspires her!

Emma

Emma always knows what the next trend will be. She pays attention to color combinations, and loves to add a small piece of jewelry as a finishing touch.

Comb

Microphone

Andrea

Andrea's personal style reflects her outgoing personality. She loves bright colors, and anything with music notes on it is a winner!

Stephanie

When Stephanie is organizing an event, she likes to look the part. She wears a tailored jacket and pretty shoes to complete her outfit—and to let everyone know who's boss!

Handbag

Wand

Mia

When Mia practices her magic, she wears this cool magician's outfit. It looks professional and dramatic—and it has a few secret pockets, too!

Olivia

Olivia is shy and practical, so her clothes are never too crazy! She likes to have pockets or a roomy handbag to keep all of her gadgets close at hand.

Bag for gadgets

Why not **think up** the perfect **hat** to go with this outfit?

You could add a **pattern** or a **picture** to reflect Emma's favorite things.

Which **colors** will you choose for the **skirt** and the **top**?

Draw an **accessory** or some **jewelry** to go with your outfit.

15

Friends Challenge

Test your knowledge on Chapter 1

Answer each question. If you need help, look back through the section.

Now you have finished the first chapter of the book, take the Friends Challenge to prove your Friends knowledge!

 1 Find the sticker that best matches the description:

This vehicle helps Emma carry medical supplies and rescue animals in the jungle.

 2 Olivia has designed a robot called...

Zorga **Zobo** **Zondo** [ ]

 3 Andrea owns a white poodle called Lady.

True **False** [ ]

4 Name this friend:

✎ _____

5 Kate wears ✎ _____

on her feet for her favorite hobby, snorkeling.

 Find the **answers** on page 97.

Now you have finished the Friends Challenge, reward yourself by filling this scene with your extra stickers!

CHAPTER 2 ✗ Heartlake City

High School
The friends always have fun at Heartlake High. Not only do they learn a variety of subjects, they make lots of new friends at school too.

Bakery
Downtown Bakery is always full of the freshest breads and cakes. On the way to school, work, or on a day out, make sure to pick up a tasty snack.

Hair Salon
To make your hair look extra special, Heartlake Hair Salon is the place to go. Ask Natasha, the director, to recommend a stylish new look for you!

Heartlake City is a wonderful place to live. There are so many places to visit and plenty of fun things to do. From pet pampering and flying lessons to horse riding and makeovers —there's so much to choose from!

Find the **stickers** at the back of the book.

Pet Salon

Pets need pampering too! Bring your pet along to the Heartlake Pet Salon for a shampoo treatment, a new look, or some new accessories. Woof!

Flying Club

Learn to fly a plane on your own at the Heartlake Flying Club. Stephanie recently got her pilot's license—she loves taking to the skies!

Vet Clinic

Bring your sick pets to the Vet Clinic. The clinic also offers to train your pet— or to take her for a walk and help her make new friends.

Stables

For a horsey day out, head to Heartlake Stables. Explore the grounds on a gentle horse, help groom and feed the foals, and improve your riding skills.

Beauty Shop

Whether you want a completely new style, or a new lipstick color, Butterfly Beauty Shop is the best place to go!

Tourist Guide
Take a tour of the city

Heartlake City is famous for its beauty. Tourists love to walk across the city and visit all the sights. Heartlake City is never boring—there are fun things to do here every single day.

What to do:

1. Ask a friend or two to join you on your tour of Heartlake City, and decide who will go first.

2. Grab some LEGO® mini-dolls, or something else to use as counters, and place them at the start position.

3. Take turns to roll a die, then move the number of spaces that are shown on the die.

4. Be the first person to reach the Shopping Mall.

5. Watch out for distractions along the way!

Read the instructions for the game, then start playing!

City Park Café

Time for a well-earned snack. City Park Café serves the best burgers in town—not to mention dessert! It also has a great view of Lake Heart.

You meet a Heartlake City local, who gives you some top sightseeing tips. **Move forward 2 spaces**.

Start

10

9

8

7

6

5

4

3

2

1

Lake Heart

Relax next to the sparkling blue water of the famous Lake Heart. Have a picnic or a barbecue, or just read a book under a shady tree.

What's that wonderful smell? **Run forward 2 spaces** and eat some fried eggs with Joanna.

Heartlake Shopping Mall

End your day of sightseeing at the mall, where you can buy a souvenir of your vacation. It's also a great place to grab a tasty pizza for supper!

Wow—a water slide! Heartlake City Pool is a great place to swim and enjoy a popsicle. **Go back 1 space** to splash around.

End

You stop to take one last look at the beautiful Heartlake City. **Miss a go** while you take some keepsake photos.

27

28

29

26

25

A nutrient-packed apple bran muffin from Downtown Bakery gives you a burst of energy. **Buzz forward 1 space**.

Ambersands Beach

With crystal clear water and soft sand, The beach is a top tourist spot. Enjoy the breeze at the Beach House, or have a go at surfing.

24

23

11

12

22

A quick paddle in the warm ocean water is very tempting. **Go back 1 space** for a lovely swim.

21

20

You become distracted by Stephanie's dance performance. **Miss a go** while you groove along.

13

Heartlake Lighthouse offers the best views of the city. Climb to the top and **roll an extra turn**.

14

19

All this walking is tiring! Luckily, Olivia offers you a ride in her speedboat. **Zoom forward 3 spaces**.

15

18

16

17

The Lighthouse
Complete the sticker jigsaw

Heartlake Lighthouse stands on the historic Kate's Island. It is named after Dark-Eyed Kate, Heartlake City's legendary pirate. Even today, the lighthouse is still in use—and there's a delicious ice cream shop next door. Mmm!

I love hanging out at the lighthouse!

Use the stickers of the lighthouse parts to put the building together.

Ice Cream Shop

Kate runs the lighthouse ice cream shop. She and her friends are always inventing new flavors—last week it was Pirate Jewel flavor!

Sunny spot

Always in the sun, but with a lovely breeze, this is the perfect place to enjoy a delicious ice cream.

Jason the seal

This friendly seal is a regular at the lighthouse. He can often be seen lounging on nearby rocks and barking playfully at visitors.

Sandy beach

Kate's Island is small, but a little beach still offers somewhere to catch a tan and build sandcastles.

Find the **stickers** at the back of the book.

Bright light

A revolving light at the top of the tower warns ships to be careful as there are hidden rocks under the water here.

Hidden secrets

Stephanie and Kate managed to find a hidden ladder that leads to secret rooms in the lighthouse tower. What will they find inside?

Stephanie and Kate

Friends Stephanie and Kate love hanging out at the lighthouse and showing tourists around.

Me too. Let's think up a new ice cream flavor!

Vines

The lighthouse has been on this island for many years. Warm, wet conditions have allowed vines to grow up the sides of the tower.

Giant ice cream

This sculpture of a giant ice cream cone entices tourists on boat tours to dock at the island for an ice-cold snack.

City Park Café

Create a new menu

City Park Café is the most popular café in Heartlake City. It is famous for its delicious food, including burgers, fries, milkshakes, pies, and cupcakes. Marie, the café owner, is always coming up with exciting new ideas for the menu.

Read about the City Park Café food and fill in the menu with your own ideas. Draw pictures of the food too.

Savory treats

For a tasty meal, look no further than Marie's Heartlake Burger and fries. They are made with fresh ingredients—and plenty of love and care.

Desserts

Marie is famous for her cakes and tasty treats. Cupcakes come in all different flavors, and Marie loves thinking up bold new combinations.

City Park Café
MENU

1 You've tasted our famous Heartlake Burger. Now try the new Exotic Burger. It comes with these toppings:

✏ _____

_____

2 Fries are always delicious. Have you tasted our fabulous pesto fries? We've just added a new flavor too:

✏ _____ fries.

3 The Brunch Salad comes with lettuce, cucumbers, tomatoes, crispy leek, and dried berries. Why not try our new Sunny Day Salad, which comes with

✏ _____

4 My favorite cupcake flavor at the moment is chocolate chilli. We have just introduced another unusual flavor: the ✏ _____

_____ cupcake.

Decorate the menu with your own **drawings**.

Shopping Mall
Find the shops at the mall

Heartlake Shopping Mall is never quiet. Bustling stores, excited shoppers, and regular events make the mall an exciting destination—and not just for shopping!

What a great day at the mall!

Read about Heartlake Shopping Mall, then find the missing stickers.

Bridal boutique

This exclusive store sells glamorous bridal gowns and beautiful jewelry. It is always up to date with the latest fashions and trends.

Beauty spa

The mall is a busy place, but the beauty spa is a calm and relaxing environment. It offers mud treatments, hair styling, and manicures.

Photo booth

There's no better way to remember a fun day out than with photos. Emma and Stephanie pose for lots of silly pictures in the mall's photo booth!

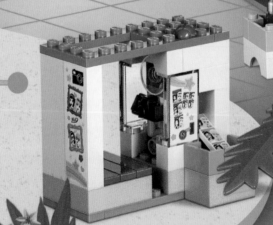

Find the **stickers** at the back of the book.

Food court

Shopping can make you hungry! Luckily, the food court serves delicious food. Emma orders an oven-baked pizza from her friend Julian.

Sports store

The sports store sells all you need for an energetic expedition: from camping supplies and skateboards to outdoor clothing. It even repairs bicycles!

Bag cart

The mobile bag cart sells handbags of all shapes and sizes. Olivia found her favorite blue and pink handbag at this cute cart.

Heartlake Shops

Create and design a new shop

Heartlake City is famous for its beautiful shopping arcades and enticing stores. Shop owners work very hard to make their shops look appealing to customers.

> Read about some of the Heartlake City shops, then design your own.

Downtown Bakery

Heartlake City's bakery is famous for its breads, cakes, and pastries. Inside the shop is a kitchen, ingredients, and plenty of baking utensils.

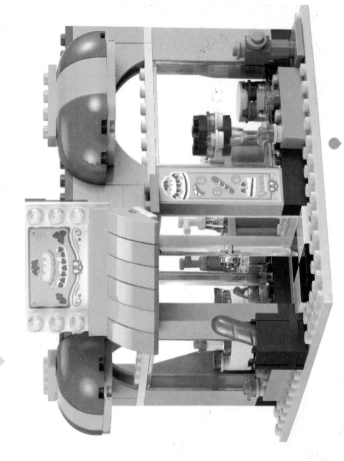

Window display

The bakery has lovely big windows which display the wonderful cake creations. It looks great—and tempts customers inside, too!

Eye-catching sign

The logo and sign for the shop should clearly show what goods or services are offered inside. It should also be bright and colorful.

Butterfly Beauty

The Butterfly Beauty Shop offers pampering and makeover services. Colorful cosmetics are displayed in the large windows, while a pretty fountain outside makes a restful sound.

What will your shop sell? **Food**? **Clothes**? A much needed service?

Choose **colors** to reflect what your shop is **selling**.

How will your shop **attract customers**?

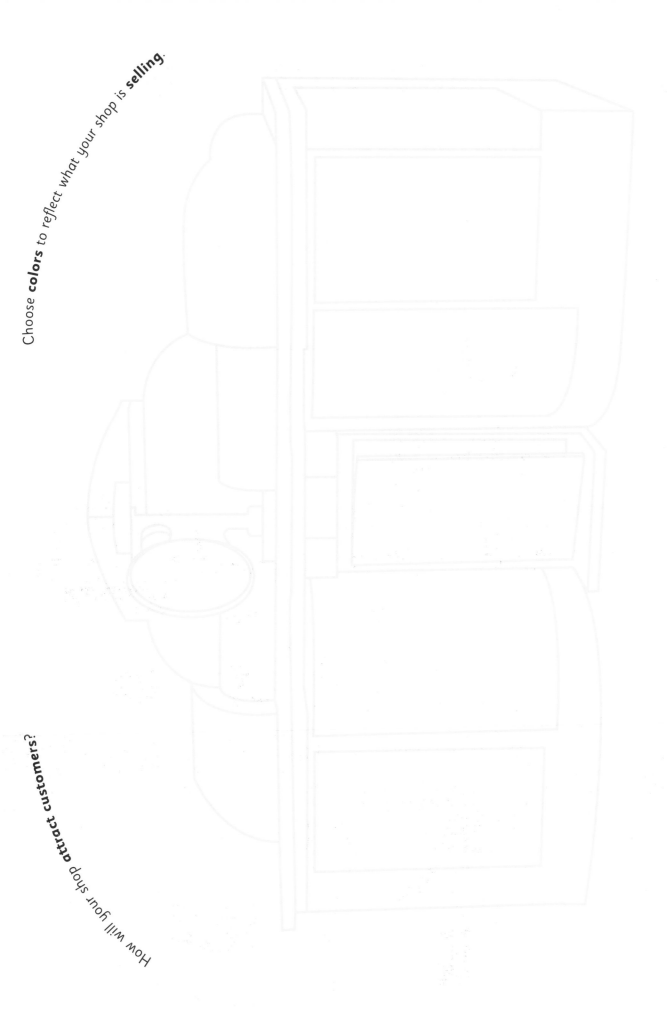

Heartlake Juice Bar

Complete the to-do list

Heartlake Juice Bar is the best place to get a delicious, fresh fruit smoothie. Naya loves working here, and she works really hard to keep the business running smoothly. She makes a list of her daily jobs to keep track of everything she needs to remember.

Read about the juice bar and choose the correct stickers to complete Naya's to-do list.

Menu

The menu displays "Smoothie Specials." Naya updates the menu every day with exciting new flavors.

Smoothie machine

The smoothie machines blend fresh fruit into a super-smooth drink. The machines need to be cleaned after each use.

Snacks

Naya prepares simple, healthy snacks—such as cranberry muffins and banana bread—for her customers to eat alongside their smoothies.

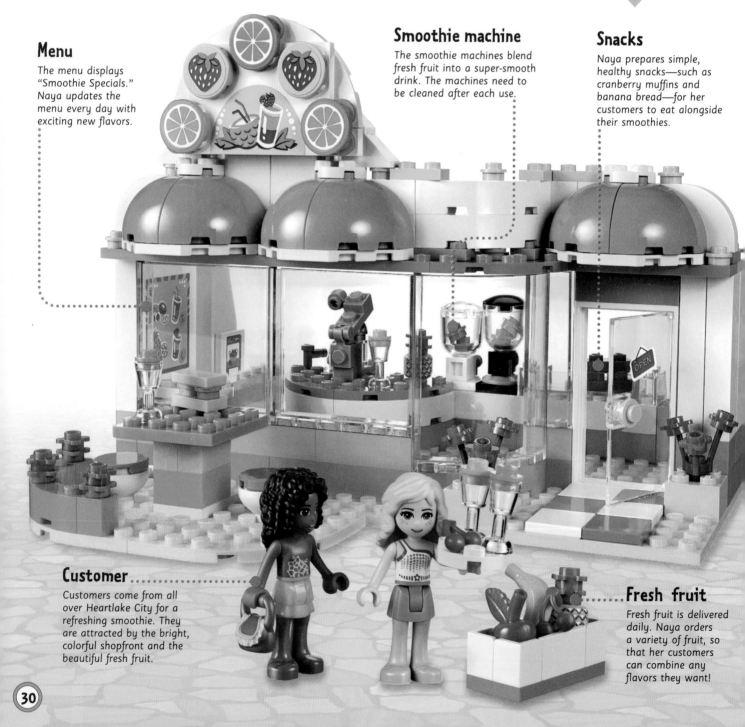

Customer

Customers come from all over Heartlake City for a refreshing smoothie. They are attracted by the bright, colorful shopfront and the beautiful fresh fruit.

Fresh fruit

Fresh fruit is delivered daily. Naya orders a variety of fruit, so that her customers can combine any flavors they want!

Naya's To-do list

1. Wash all the fruit carefully.

2. Clean the machines and make sure they are working well.

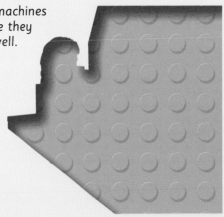

3. Think up new and exciting flavor combinations for the menu.

4. Take your customers' orders at the till and give them the correct change.

5. Be careful not to spill the smoothies as you bring them to the customers.

6. Take some time to enjoy the smoothies with your customers!

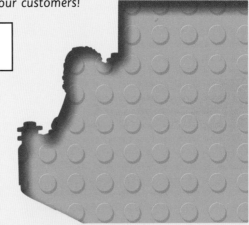

Find the **stickers** at the back of the book.

Put a **tick** in each box once you find the stickers.

31

Friends Challenge
Test your knowledge on Chapter 2

Answer each question. If you need help, look back through the section.

Now you have finished the second chapter of the book, take the Friends Challenge to prove your Friends knowledge!

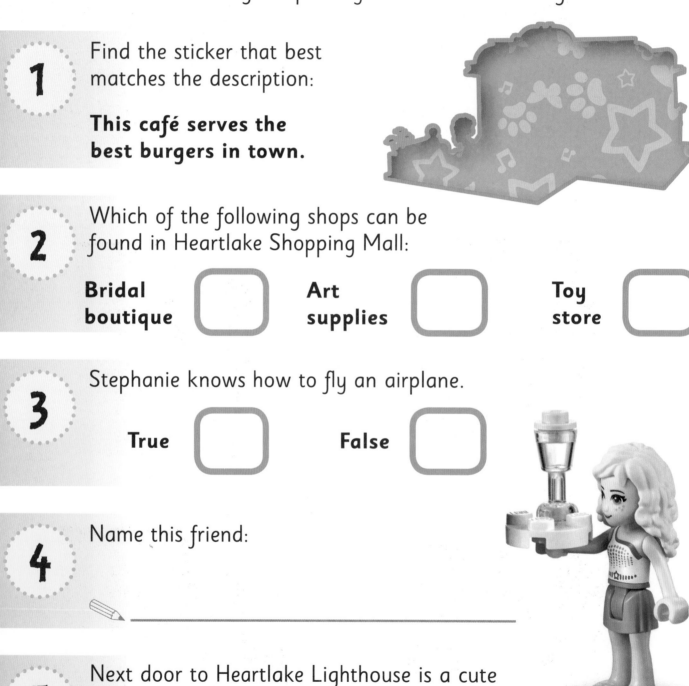

1 Find the sticker that best matches the description:

This café serves the best burgers in town.

2 Which of the following shops can be found in Heartlake Shopping Mall:

Bridal boutique ☐   **Art supplies** ☐   **Toy store** ☐

3 Stephanie knows how to fly an airplane.

True ☐   **False** ☐

4 Name this friend:

✎ _____

5 Next door to Heartlake Lighthouse is a cute

little ✎ _____ _____ shop.

Find the **answers** on page 97.

Now you have finished the Friends Challenge, reward yourself by filling this scene with your extra stickers!

Andrea, Olivia, Stephanie, Mia, and Emma love animals. They take care of their pets, ride horses, care for sick animals at the vet, and explore the jungle to discover animals in their natural habitats.

Charlie

Cute puppy Charlie follows his owner, Mia, everywhere. The only time he'll leave her side is if he spots a bunny —he can't resist chasing them!

Mocca and Fame

Mocca and his young foal Fame live on Sunshine Ranch. Fame is curious about everything, just like his dad. They love to explore the ranch together.

Flame

Flame is a friendly tiger cub. She lives in a lovely purple and gold temple in the jungle and she loves it when the friends come to visit her.

Kiki

Emma's green parrot Kiki often leaves her perch to fly around Heartlake City. She keeps everyone entertained with funny words she has learned.

Find the **stickers** at the back of the book.

Daisy

Stephanie rescued Daisy from a parking lot! She takes care of this gorgeous white bunny every day, cleaning out her hutch and feeding her carrots.

Hazel

Hazel is a hungry little squirrel, who is always foraging for nuts and seeds. Andrea has made friends with Hazel, and often brings her food.

Cora

Cora is a mischievous orange cat. She likes to slink around and squint her eyes at everyone. The best way to make friends is to squint back at her!

Sheen and Milo

Sheen and her brother Milo are two dolphins who live off the coast of Heartlake City. They enjoy playing pranks on their sea creature friends.

Home Sweet Home

Create a new home for a lost animal

All animals are different. Their homes must have the right environment, materials, and food for their individual needs. Sometimes, the friends rescue lost animals and find them perfect new homes.

Read the information about different animals' needs, then create a new home for a lost turtle.

Penguins

Penguins love being cold, eating fish, and swimming, so they need a home near water. Penguins are fun-loving, too, so a water slide is a great feature in their home!

Lambs

Newborn lambs are playful, but clumsy. They need a warm, sheltered home where they can play safely. Stephanie built her lamb a cozy hut with a water pump for washing.

Fawns

Fawns are baby deer. They are energetic and need lots of space to run around. Most fawns live in the woods, where they eat grass, herbs, berries, and acorns.

Bears

Bears are quiet, private creatures. They usually build their homes in dark, cool places, like caves. They eat plants and catch fish that leap out from nearby rivers or streams.

Found: A Lost Turtle

Andrea found a lost turtle. She wants
to build it a new home. Can you help?
Turtles:

- *love exploring*
- *splash around in water most of the time*
- *lounge in the sun, but need plenty of shade*
- *eat crayfish and fruit, so need to be near
these foods*

Where will the turtle's home be? Near the **sea**, a **stream**, or a **waterfall**?

Draw **lightly** with a **pencil** before you use **colored pens** or **pencils**.

Will the turtle's home have any **fun features** for the turtle to play with?

Charity Event
Help organize a charity event

Mia decides to raise money for a new animal medical unit, so all her friends jump at the chance to help. Planning a charity music concert is no easy task. Especially when five very different personalities all want to get involved!

Learn about each friend's skills and talents, then find the correct stickers.

The boss

Stephanie is never far from her phone. She loves **organizing** (and secretly loves being the boss). Stephanie is a pro at making lists and remembering which **tasks** still need to be done.

Animal lover

Kind Mia is always coming up with new ways to help her four-legged friends. She devotes lots of time and **effort** into developing her ideas and addressing all the **issues** and information she thinks are important.

Design wonder

Emma's **creative** side bursts out at every opportunity. As soon as someone mentions an event, Emma is already thinking about the eye-catching posters, **flyers**, and decorations she can design on her laptop.

Techno whizz

Olivia's scientific mind always helps her invent **solutions** to various problems. She loves coming up with computer programs and websites that have clever, **easy-to-use** functions.

Music lover

Dramatic and energetic, Andrea knows that no event is complete without **music**! She loves singing her own songs, and she always knows what sort of **attraction** is perfect for a specific event.

1. Planning

*The first task when planning the concert is to send out invitations! Whoever is in charge needs to be very **organized** and good at making **lists**. They must also keep track of what jobs have been done.*

2. Advertising

*Designing a great **poster** or flyer will make people want to come to the concert. The poster must be **eye-catching**, and include details such as where and when.*

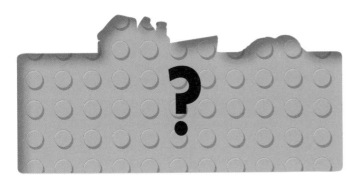

3. Informing

*So what's the event all about then? People need to know. This information must be carefully **researched** and **presented** to make the guests understand why an animal medical unit is needed.*

4. Entertaining

*The charity music concert has to be interesting—but also **fun**! The entertainment is really important because it makes the guests **happy** and encourages them to donate.*

5. Donating

*The concert should be a great night out, but remember: it's also about raising money for the animal medical unit. There should be an **easy** way for the guests to donate, perhaps using a secure **website**.*

Find the **stickers** at the back of the book.

Find the **answers** on page 97.

Heartlake Horses

Draw a new horse

The many horses of Heartlake City have one thing in common: they need to be treated with love and respect. Apart from that, they are all different! From coat color and competitiveness, to favorite food and personality, no two horses are the same.

Read about the horses. Then draw your dream horse!

Horse Facts

Eye color: Blue
Favorite food: Apples
Personality: Leader

Blaize

Obedient horse Blaize has a snow-white coat, mane, and tail. He is happy to wear a blue saddle and secure bridle, so his owners can ride on him.

Horse Facts

Eye color: Blue
Favorite food: Hay
Personality: Mischievous

Ruby

Ruby has a soft reddish-brown coat, tail, and mane. She wears a pretty purple saddle and is proud of her blue second prize rosette.

Horse Facts

Eye color: Brown
Favorite food: Berries
Personality: Sensible

Major

Gentle Major has a thick black mane, a sleek chestnut coat, and a white blaze over his nose. He always feels his best when his friend Robert ties an aqua bow to his tail.

Will your horse's **mane** and **tail** be the same color as its **coat**?

Will your horse have a **saddle**? Or something else?

Accessories

Name: _____

Favorite
food: _____

Favorite
color: _____

Personality: _____

The Dog Show
Design a new obstacle course

It's time for the annual Heartlake Dog Show! Proud dog-owners must help their clever pups complete a fun obstacle course. If the dog performs well enough, it could win a prize!

Roundabout

Each dog must take a turn on the roundabout, sitting still as it turns round once, then getting off again.

Read about the dog show obstacles. Next, add stickers to design your course. Then draw a route between the obstacles.

Start

Find the dog show **stickers** at the back of the book.

Runway

Show off your dog to the judges on this runway! Help your pooch walk there and back—and look her best!

Seesaw

Lead your pup up the seesaw, helping him stay balanced as it tips down. Then help him walk off the other side.

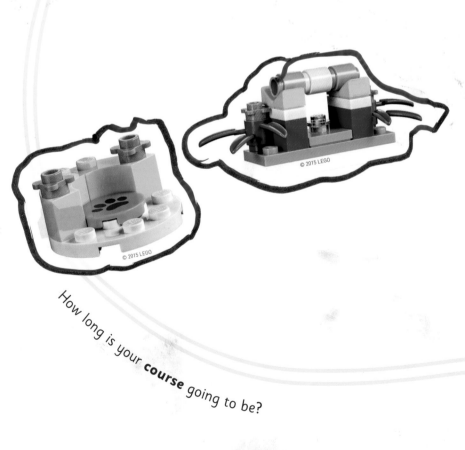

How long is your course going to be?

Obstacle cones

Time to show how well your dog listens! Help her in and out of the obstacle cones —the faster the better!

Water jump

Help your dog leap over the small puddle. He might be tempted to have a splash, but try not to let him!

Hurdle

Your dog must jump over the hurdle without knocking it down. It's very tiring. Good luck!

Where are your **obstacles** going to go?

Use a **pencil** to draw the **route** between the stickers.

Finish

Animal Rescue

Finish the comic strip

The jungle can be dangerous for small animals. There are many places where an animal could get stuck or trapped. Luckily, the friends are always on the lookout for animals who need help.

Rescue team—on our way!

What **title** will you give your story?

Read the story and then write and draw the ending.

Use these images to help you.

Flame

Tiger cub Flame is small, but she is very adventurous!

Rescue ring

This floating ring is often used in water rescue missions.

Oh no! Flame the tiger cub is trapped in the middle of a fast-flowing river.

Emma jumps onto the First Aid Bike and races to the river.

Hold on Flame, I'm on my way!

Stephanie hears about the rescue mission on her walkie talkie. She steers her raft boat up the river toward Flame.

Draw lightly with a **pencil** before you use **colored pens** or **pencils**.

Andrea takes the zip line down from the Jungle Rescue Base.

This is WAY faster than walking!

Mia pilots the superfast Rescue Helicopter. She can see Flame from the air.

There she is! I need somewhere to land.

Olivia grabs a rescue ring and hurries to the riverbank.

Which of the friends will get there first?

THE END!

How will the story **end**? You **decide!**

Helicopter

The helicopter can speed to the rescue, but it needs a safe place to land.

Raft boat

The raft boat is very useful for dangerous water rescue missions.

First Aid Bike

The First Aid Bike can speed through even the narrowest of jungle paths.

Medical kit

The friends carry medical supplies whenever they go on a rescue mission.

The Vet Clinic

Help the vet treat the sick animals

Oh no! Your beloved pet isn't feeling well. Time to visit the vet. At the Vet Clinic, the vet will have a look at the problem and come up with a treatment plan. Your pet will be back to normal in no time!

Read the information, then fill in the vet's report.

Be on time
The vet is usually very busy, so it is important to be on time for your appointment. That way, your pet will receive the best care.

Cuts and scratches
Cuts and scratches need to be cleaned properly with warm water. The vet will apply a soothing cream to stop the pain, then put on a band-aid to let the wound heal.

Fractures and sprains
For broken bones and sprained ankles, the animal should rest the injured arm or leg. The vet will put a plaster cast on broken bones and wrap a soft bandage around sprains.

Colds and infections
For colds and infections, the vet will tell your pet to have lots of rest and take medicine. For eye infections, the medicine will be eye drops and for ear infections, it will be ear drops.

Examination table
The vet examines each animal very carefully. This helps her decide what is wrong, and what is the best way to make the animal feel better.

Phone the vet
If you are worried about your pet, always phone the vet. She is happy to help!

Vet Report

Name: Satin

Animal: Seal

Problem: A cold

Treatment: Have lots of rest and take medicine.

Name: Maxie

Animal:

Problem: Sprained ankle

Treatment:

Name: Jazz

Animal:

Problem: Ear infection

Treatment:

Name: Jojo

Animal:

Problem: Sharp scratch on paw

Treatment:

Fill in the missing **information** on the vet's report.

Friends Challenge
Test your knowledge on Chapter 3

Answer each question. If you need help, look back through the section.

Now you have finished the third chapter of the book, take the Friends Challenge to prove your Friends knowledge!

1 Find the sticker that best matches the description:

This cute hedgehog came to the Vet Clinic because she had a sharp scratch on her paw.

2 The friends race to rescue tiger cub Flame, who is trapped in a...

swamp   cave   river

3 Penguins love being warm.

True   False

4 Name this friend:

 _____

5 Mocca and his son Fame are two of the

 _____ who live on Sunshine Ranch.

Find the **answers** on page 97.

Now you have finished the Friends Challenge, reward yourself by filling this scene with your extra stickers!

CHAPTER 4 ✽ Great Outdoors

Find the **stickers** at the back of the book.

Jungle friends

Mia explores the jungle, keeping an eye out for lost or injured animals. She loves feeding hungry lion cubs and helping them find their home.

Barbecue

There's nothing better than a barbecue after a long hike. Olivia and Joanna fry some eggs before heading into their caravan for the night.

Windsurfing

Stephanie's idea of fun usually involves lots of hard work! Windsurfing is an amazing sport, but it has taken Stephanie many hours of practice to become this good.

Jungle rescue

An injured panda has been spotted from the Jungle Rescue Base watchtower. Stephanie slides down to the boat to sail to the rescue.

The friends love going on adventures to exciting places. From the fresh air of Heartlake City's sunny beaches to the humid jungle—there's never a dull moment to be found on an outdoor adventure.

Horse riding

Whenever Emma wants to practice her riding skills, she loads Robin, her gorgeous horse, into her trailer and sets off for the glorious countryside.

Poolside fun

Andrea and Isabella enjoy a cool drink in the hot tub at Heartlake City Pool. Then they will dive into the main pool with a big splash!

Cycling

Olivia and Nicole load up their bikes with a picnic lunch and head off to explore the shady paths of the Whispering Woods.

At the beach

Andrea enjoys a day at the beach. She builds sandcastles, listens to music in the shade, and keeps a lookout for boats with her telescope.

The Ocean

Write your own blog post

Heartlake City has lots of beautiful beaches. The ocean is full of incredible wildlife, including fish, crabs, seahorses, and dolphins. Maya has won a contest to join a dolphin research mission aboard a Dolphin Cruiser.

Read about the research mission, then write a guest blog post for Andrea's Alley about it.

Dolphin Cruiser

The impressive Dolphin Cruiser has three decks: the bottom deck houses all the research equipment and the middle deck is the living quarters, with beds, a small kitchen (called a galley), and a bathroom. The captain sits on the top deck, which has all his navigational equipment.

Life on board

At first, Maya is surprised by how cramped everything is aboard the Dolphin Cruiser. She soon learns that ships only have limited space, so everything must be as compact as possible. At least the beds are comfortable!

Hi dolphins!

To observe the dolphins up close, Andrew takes Maya for a water-skiing ride. It is such fun, especially getting so close to two beautiful dolphins. Maya is soaked through at the end, but it has been her favorite part of the mission!

Time to relax!

The research mission keeps Maya very busy. She really enjoys recording her observations of the dolphins, but she also loves the times when she and Mia get to relax with ice creams on the sundeck!

ANDREA'S ALLEY

Welcome to my blog! I hope you enjoy all the interesting
articles written by me and my guest reporters.
Love, Andrea x

DOLPHINS SPOTTED!

THE DOLPHIN RESEARCH MISSION: MAYA'S REPORT

_____

_____

_____

_____

_____

_____

_____

_____

_____

_____

THE RESEARCH CREW.

Draw a **picture** to go with your story.

Write about the **exciting things** that happened.

The Jungle
Rescue the lost animals

The jungle is a big place, full of winding paths and thick trees. It's not surprising that animals sometimes get lost. Kind Mia often heads into the jungle, looking to help lost animals.

Help Mia rescue the lost animals as she travels through the maze. Add a sticker as you reach each animal.

Juliet

This cute orangutan swings from vines in search of bananas. But there are no bananas in this part of the jungle.

Blu

Baby bear Blu has wandered far from his cave. He was searching for berries, but now he can't find his way home.

Animal lover

Mia is passionate about animals. She cares about their feelings and wants to look after them. She spends a lot of time in the jungle, caring for her animal friends.

Start

Java

Java has hurt one of her wings, so she can't fly. Luckily, this macaw can squawk loudly—Mia will soon find her.

End

Jungle Rescue Base

Mia and her friends plan their rescue missions from the Jungle Rescue Base. It has a tall watchtower for spotting lost animals, a research center, and a mobile medical station to treat any injuries.

Bamboo

Cute panda Bamboo is being cared for at the Jungle Rescue Base. He loves climbing trees, but he has climbed too far.

Bobbi

Bobbi the lion cub lives on the grassy savannah. She was on her way to visit her jungle friends when she got lost. Help!

Hot Air Balloon

Design a poster

The Hot Air Balloon is a new addition to the Heartlake City tourist scene. It is an eco-friendly way to explore the skies over the city—and there is nothing more exhilarating than flying in a giant balloon!

Nothing beats a hot air balloon ride!

Read about the Hot Air Balloon, then draw a picture on the poster and fill in the blanks.

Clearspring Falls

This little-known beauty spot is quiet and secluded. It is nestled on a ledge near the Clearspring Mountains—and is reachable only by air.

Hot Air Balloon

A journey in the Hot Air Balloon is an incredible way to see Heartlake City from above. Relax in the basket as the hot air makes the balloon lift off from the ground!

Picnic

There's nothing better than a picnic after an exciting Hot Air Balloon ride! Noah brings fresh pastries and Andrea cooks her specialty: roasted marshmallows.

Andrea and Noah

Andrea and her friend Noah are learning to pilot the Hot Air Balloon. At first, they disagree about lots of things, but now they are great friends.

Draw a **picture** of a hot air balloon ride on your poster.

You could add the words "**Brand New!**" or "**Amazing New Adventure!**" at the top.

Hot Air Balloon Rides!

Join us for an amazing adventure in the air!

Fly high and enjoy magical views of ✎ _____
City. Land at the top of ✎ _____ Falls
and enjoy a perfect picnic of fresh pastries and roasted
✎ _____ .

Call Andrea and ✎ _____ to book your spot!

Sunshine Ranch

Complete Mia's scrapbook

Mia's grandparents live on a country farm called Sunshine Ranch. They grow their own fruit and vegetables and look after lots of animals. Mia likes to visit at the weekends.

Read about Sunshine Ranch, then complete Mia's scrapbook using stickers and your own drawings.

Ranch
Sunshine Ranch is a large farmhouse in a lovely countryside location. The horse's stables are on the ground floor, while the living area is upstairs.

Mia
Mia loves visiting her grandparents' ranch. She helps out with jobs—and makes plenty of time to play with the animals!

Liza
Liza often joins her cousin Mia at Sunshine Ranch. Gardening is Liza's favorite hobby, but she also loves riding the horses.

Horses
Three horses live on Sunshine Ranch: white Blaize, chestnut Mocca, and their adorable newborn foal, Fame.

A Day at Sunshine Ranch

Liza and I started the day with some breakfast in the ranch's sunny kitchen. Pancakes and cherries. Yum!

I loved collecting fresh eggs from the chicken coop. We found six!

My favorite part of the day was grooming the horses. Blaize loved it when I brushed her coat. She stood so still for me!

It was nice to hang out with Liza again. We had a lovely picnic under the shade of the cherry tree.

As the sun was setting, I went for a ride on Mocca, a beautiful chestnut brown horse. What a perfect day!

Mia x

Use your imagination to **draw** the final picture.

Monkey Mayhem

Find the animals and their hidden objects

The monkeys of the jungle have always enjoyed playing tricks on their human friends. Now, some of their animal friends are joining in too. Lots of medical supplies (and bananas) have recently gone missing.

Read the captions about the jungle animals and find the sticker that best fits the space.

Romeo

Romeo loves bananas more than anything else! Whenever this monkey spots one, he swipes it and swings away to find a good hiding place for it.

?

_____ Bananas

How many hidden objects can you find? Write the numbers in the boxes.

Find the **answers** on page 97.

Find the **stickers** at the back of the book.

Bubbles

Green turtle Bubbles might be old and wise, but he still likes playing pranks. He sometimes hides thermometers to make the jungle rescue team laugh!

 _____ Thermometers

Goldie

As a bird, Goldie has an easy time of snatching objects. She simply picks up medical kits in her beak and flies them away to a hiding place!

_____ Medical kits

Zip

Zip might be a tiny, slimy frog, but he can't resist hiding every stethoscope he finds. He drags them along, leaving a slippery trail behind him.

 _____ Stethoscopes

Hoo hoo ha ha! I go bananas for ... bananas!

Help is at Hand

Find the friend who can help out

For every problem, there's a solution. Going on adventures and hanging out with friends is always fun—but if there's something missing, a friend will always be around to lend a hand.

Read about each situation, then find the sticker which will help solve the problem.

Ocean fun

Olivia enjoys taking her speedboat out for a ride on the ocean waves. However, it is important to stay safe in the water.

Safe swimming

Lifeguards stand on a raised platform and keep a look out for anyone in trouble at the beach.

Peaceful nature

The Whispering Woods are full of wildlife, like these adorable squirrels and pretty flowers. Nature lovers need a quiet retreat where they can enjoy nature without disturbing it.

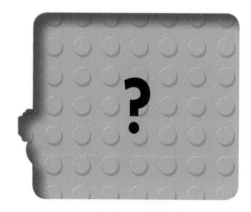

Secluded cabin

The Mountain Hut is a quiet place. It is so peaceful here that you can observe nature without scaring the animals.

Hot summer's day

Where better to enjoy a sunny day than Ambersands Beach? If only Olivia and Kate had something cold and sweet to eat.

Sleepover

Hooray—it's sleepover time! Mia and Emma love hanging out, but they are getting a bit hungry. How can they get some supper delivered?

Sports training

Stephanie and Matthew are tired and thirsty after a long sports practice. They could do with an ice-cold drink to rehydrate themselves!

Beach refreshments

Selling ice creams on the beach is a winning idea. Everyone wants a frozen treat from the ice cream bike!

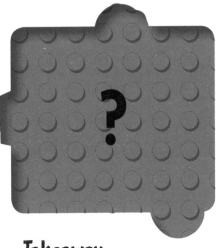

Takeaway

Did somebody say pizza? This friend holds the record for fastest pizza delivery!

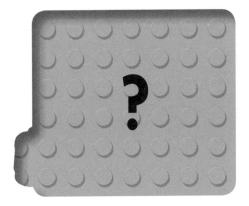

A welcome drink

There's nothing better than an ice-cold glass of lemonade when you're thirsty!

Find the **stickers** at the back of the book.

Find the **answers** on page 97.

Friends Challenge
Test your knowledge on Chapter 4

Answer each question. If you need help, look back through the section.

Now you have finished the fourth chapter of the book, take the Friends Challenge to prove your Friends knowledge!

1 Find the sticker that best matches the description:

Mia's grandparents live on this farm. They have horses, bunnies, and chickens.

2 In her spare time, Stephanie...

works at the café   **is a lifeguard**   **goes windsurfing**

3 Bubbles the turtle has started playing pranks on his human friends.

True   **False**

4 Name this friend:

 _____

5 Maya joined her friends Mia and Andrew on a

 _____ research mission.